GOING ALONG THE EMIGRANT TRAILS

BY BARBARA FIFER

FARCOUNTRY
PRESS

HELENA, MONTANA

Acknowledgments

Miles and miles of thanks to Robert J. Moore, Jr., for making sure I "saw the elephant" in proper focus, to Caroline Patterson at Farcountry Press for her endless good cheer and clever ideas, and to Shirley Machonis and Lisa Mee for an excellent design.

ISBN-13: 978-1-56037-354-4
ISBN-10: 1-56037-354-7

Library of Congress Cataloging-in-Publication Data

Fifer, Barbara.
 Going along the emigrant trails / by Barbara Fifer.
 p. cm.
 ISBN-13: 978-1-56037-354-4
 1. Overland Trails. 2. Pioneers—West (U.S.) 3. Frontier and pioneer life—West (U.S.) 4. West (U.S.)—Description and travel. I. Title.
 F593.F54 2006
 978'.02—dc22

 2005023501

For more information on our books, write Farcountry Press, P.O. Box 5630, Helena, MT 59604; call (800) 821-3874; or visit www.farcountrypress.com.

Created, produced, and designed in the United States. Printed in China.

10 09 08 07 06   1 2 3 4 5 6

Document Sources:

Bailey, Theodore A. July 22, 1866 Diary. Theodore A. Bailey Diary. SC1438. Montana Historical Society Archives.

Cowan, Emma Carpenter. Reminiscence. 1902. SC576. MHS Archives.

Fletcher, Ellen. Letter, n.d., and letter May 23, 1866. Ellen "Nellie" Fletcher Papers. SC78. MHS Archives

Knight, Amelia Stewart. Diary. The Oregon Trail Diaries. http://www.isu.edu/%7Etrinmich/00.n.dairies.html

Owen, Richard. July 7 and July 12 Diary. 1864. Richard Owen Diaries. SC613. MHS Archives.

Pringle, Catherine Sager. Across the Plains in 1844. Whitefish, Montana: Kessenger Publishing, 2004.

Zemmer, Mollie. Letter. Used by permission of Sherry Fleischer.

All excerpts are printed as they were originally written, which may include misspellings and grammatical errors.

Photo and Illustration Credits:

Front cover, illustration, The Rocky Mountains by Currier and Ives, courtesy of the Bancroft Library, University of California, Berkeley

title page and interior page borders, illustrations by Robert Rath

back cover, George Lane, Helena Independent Record.

back cover, illustration courtesy of Culver Pictures

p. 4, Approaching Chimney Rock by William Henry Jackson, courtesy of Scotts Bluff National Monument

p. 5, illustration by Frezeny and Tavernier

p. 6, photo courtesy of L. Tom Perry Special Collections, Harold B. Lee Library, Brigham Young University, Provo, Utah

p. 7, Westport Landing by William Henry Jackson, courtesy of Scotts Bluff National Monument

p. 9, photo courtesy of American Heritage Center, University of Wyoming

p. 11, illustration courtesy of Culver Pictures

p. 12, photo courtesy of Denver Public Library, Western History Collection, X-218-3

p. 13, Manifest Destiny by John Gast, courtesy of Library of Congress, Prints and Photographs Division, LC-USZC4-668

p. 14-15, map illustrations by Robert Rath

p. 16, 17, and 18–19, illustrations by Robert Rath

p. 19, photo by Solomon Butcher, courtesy of Denver Public Library, Western History Collection, X-21805

p. 21, Mormon Party Near Fort Bridger by William Henry Jackson, courtesy of Scotts Bluff National Monument

p. 23, photo by Joseph Collier, courtesy of Denver Public Library, Western History Collection, C-7

p. 24, illustration by Robert Rath

p. 25, photo by Fred Pflughoft

p. 26, photo courtesy of Culver Pictures

p. 27, Dutch oven illustration by Robert Rath

p. 27, photo courtesy of Nebraska State Historical Society, Photographic Collections, RG3314

p. 30, photo courtesy of Picture History

p. 31, sheet music courtesy of Culver Pictures

p. 32, photo courtesy of L. Tom Perry Special Collections, Harold B. Lee Library, BYU, Provo, Utah, MSS P176

p. 36, Mormon Ferry painting by Ray Blaha, courtesy of Fort Caspar Museum

p. 37, illustration courtesy of Culver Pictures

p. 38-39, illustrations by Robert Rath

p. 40, photo courtesy of American Heritage Center, University of Wyoming

p. 41, photo courtesy of Denver Public Library, Western History Collection, X-21874

p. 42-43, map illustrations by Robert Rath

p. 44, photo courtesy of Montana Historical Society, 955-982

p. 46, photo courtesy of Picture History

Contents

WHO WERE THE EMIGRANTS?

Emigrant wagons approach Chimney Rock.

Westward Ho!

Imagine that you and your family are moving away from everything you know—your house, your friends, your town—and heading west in a covered wagon to "the Oregon country" or to California or Utah.

These are lands you have only heard about in stories. Some say it will be a place of plenty, where land is good for crops, where the rain is steady, and where gold sparkles in the streams. There are other stories about unfriendly people, harsh climates, and starvation, but you try not to listen to those.

You and your family are moving across the country on a path with no signs except natural landmarks, and certainly no traffic lights. Your

U.S. WEST

4

motel room is a covered wagon, your restaurant is the food you carry or the game you shoot along the way. Your journey will last four months if you are lucky. You hope that you make it alive.

Here I am sitting on a roll of rubber blankets surrounded by my household goods. Everything is torn up and packed, only waiting to have things put aboard the wagons. We have got a trunk of bread and soft ginger cake etc. packed, or rather a small quantity of the said article packed in the trunk. Half past twelve in the wagon, bound for Montana...I have my calicao wrapper in the wagon, a large bib apron made of that blue calico, and a new green gingham sun—bonnet, so you see I am armed and equipped.

—ELLEN "NELLIE" GORDON FLETCHER, A 24-YEAR-OLD BRIDE WHO ACCOMPANIED HER NEW HUSBAND TO HIGHLAND, MONTANA IN 1866

Headin' West

This is just what the emigrants did. From 1841 to the mid-1860s, about 350,000 Americans sold their homes and farms and moved by land to the western United States, the largest peacetime mass migration in history. The word **migration** means moving from one place to another. During that same time, nearly the same number went by ship to California.

The first people were mostly farmers seeking free land in Oregon and Utah. Then, beginning in 1849, the discovery of gold drew others to California. Gold and silver finds drew people to Colorado, Idaho, and Montana in the 1850s and 1860s. Most of the gold-seekers were men who hoped to make their fortunes and return home. Mormons heading for Utah sought religious freedom. Everyone wanted to make better lives for their families.

Most people who went west were farmers, or skilled workers like blacksmiths and carpenters. Others worked for their passage, driving teams or tending livestock. Servants traveled with their employers. A small number of African-American slaves made the trip to Oregon and California with their owners. Slavery was outlawed in the Oregon country in 1844, however, and in California six years later.

Mormon emigrant children in the 1860s.

Moving Costs

Buying food, a wagon, and a team of horses was not cheap. It cost from $12,600 to $27,000 in today's money. Many people sold their farms or small businesses to get the money.

A Long Journey

Going to Oregon or California took at least four or five months. Some travelers ran into bad weather or other difficulties that stretched their travel to six or even seven months.

Oregon Country or Oregon Territory?

Some emigrants said they were going to "Oregon country" and some said "Oregon Territory." The name they used for this land depended on when they went there.

Before the U.S.-Canadian border was created in 1846, "Oregon country" went from what is now northern California through the southern halves of British Columbia and Alberta.

In 1848, Oregon Territory was created. At that time, it reached from east of the Rocky Mountains, in today's Montana, all the way to the Pacific Ocean. The southern border was the same as it is now, and the northern border was where today's Washington–British Columbia border is.

A Family Trip

The emigrants traveled in groups of wagons called wagon trains. People of all ages made the trip, from small children to grandparents and, sometimes, babies were born along the way. In the 1840s, half of the emigrants traveled in family groups. Later gold prospectors were mostly men. Some sent for their families; others hoped to find enough gold to return home and buy a farm.

WATCH FOR WAGON TRAINS

In Good Company

Some emigrants formed groups, called "companies," in their home towns. These groups created and ran the wagon train, electing officers and setting rules. They collected money to hire the train's guide or to pay for other shared expenses. Company names often described where the members were from or where they were going, or both. Some actual company names were Wisconsin Blues, Buckeye Roamers, and California Overland and Pikes Peak Express Company.

A trip from the east to Montana in 1864 or "crossing the plains" in western parlance is very unlike a similar trip of today...at least three months of time was required...All who have made the trip [said it was] rough and wearysome; to me, a girl of ten, it was an ideal one....

I enjoyed beyond measure the gypsy style of travel, journeying toward the setting sun...sleeping at night in the great white-capped wagons that were drawn by gentle horses by day...Later, seeing the indian for the first-time, bartering for beads, learning to ride horseback on an indian pony, even the hot dry plains and scanty vegetation could not dim such delights.

—FROM "REMINISCENCES OF A PIONEER LIFE: FIRST IMPRESSIONS OF WONDERLAND" BY EMMA CARPENTER COWAN, IN WHICH SHE DESCRIBED HER TRIP TO MONTANA TERRITORY IN 1864

Emigrant or Immigrant?

What's the difference between an emigrant and an immigrant? An emigrant is someone who is *moving away* from a place. In U.S. history, people who traveled the westward trails were called emigrants because they were leaving their home states. An immigrant is someone who is *coming to* a new place to live. Immigrants are the people who come to the United States from other nations.

Turnarounds:

About ten percent of emigrants who began the trip west changed their minds and headed back home. They got the nickname "turnarounds." As they returned along the trail, they told the other emigrants about the trail ahead. Some told exaggerated stories about Indian attacks and other troubles. Guidebooks and newspapers warned emigrants not to believe everything that turnarounds said.

Westport Landing, a "jumping off" point.

Jumping Off Into the Unknown

Some emigrants gathered at "jumping-off places" along the Missouri River to buy and pack their wagons and to join wagon-train companies. When they drove away, they felt like they were jumping off the edge of the known world. Today these little villages have become cities or parts of larger cities.

Different groups often used different jumping-off spots: Mormons usually departed from Council Bluffs, Iowa, while California gold-rushers headed out from St. Joseph, Missouri. Many emigrants started out from Independence, Missouri, and Omaha, Nebraska, was a main jumping-off spot until 1861.

The First Wagon Train

The first wagon train to California, the Western Emigrant Society, started out in May 1841. The 64 men and 1 woman of this company had no guide or guidebook. All they knew was that California was west of Missouri.

Fortunately, they joined a wagon train heading for Montana and led by experienced mountain man Thomas Fitzpatrick. When they reached Soda Springs in today's Idaho, the two trains split up and went their separate ways.

The group continuing to California now included 31 men and 1 woman. They argued about routes, got  lost, and began to run out of food. Broken wagons were abandoned and oxen were eaten. In mid-September, the emigrants abandoned their wagons in eastern Nevada and walked to California, which they reached on October 31, 1841, nearly six months after their trip had started!

How Did They Know the Way?

Some wagon trains used a guidebook, map, and compass to find their way. In later years, wheel ruts helped show the emigrants where wagons had traveled.

UNKNOWN ROUTE AHEAD

When Does a Territory Become a State?

After the United States' original 13 colonies, areas had to apply to become territories before they could become states. Some of the areas the emigrants traveled through were territories, and some had no government at all.

The following are the dates when territories and states were created:

Area	Territory	State
California	*	1850
Colorado	1861	1876
Idaho	1863	1890
Iowa	1838	1846
Kansas	1854	1861
Missouri	1812	1821
Montana	1864	1889
Nebraska	1854	1867
Nevada	1861	1864
Oregon	1848	1859
Utah	1851	1896
Washington	1853	1889

*California was never a territory. Mexico ceded the land to the United States in 1848, and two years later, Congress accepted California as a state.

Other wagon trains hired guides who knew the trails. These guides often were former "mountain men," who had worked trapping beaver in the Rocky Mountains from the 1820s to 1840s and knew the best routes for wagon trains. They knew where to find good grass for the teams and safe drinking water. They knew where to ford rivers and where to cross the mountains.

We waited several days at the Missouri River. Many friends came that far to see the emigrants start on their long journey, and there was much sadness at the parting, and a sorrowful company crossed the Missouri that bright spring morning. The motion of the wagon made us all sick, and it was weeks before we got used to the seasick motion.

Soon everything went smooth and our train made steady head-way...There were several musical instruments among the emigrants, and these sounded clearly on the evening air when camp was made and merry talk and laughter resounded from almost every camp-fire.

—From *Across the Plains in 1844* by Catherine Sager Pringle

At Parting of the Ways in Wyoming, emigrants could head southwest toward Fort Bridger or take a cut-off trail on the right.

2

WHY WERE THE EMIGRANTS LEAVING THEIR HOMES?

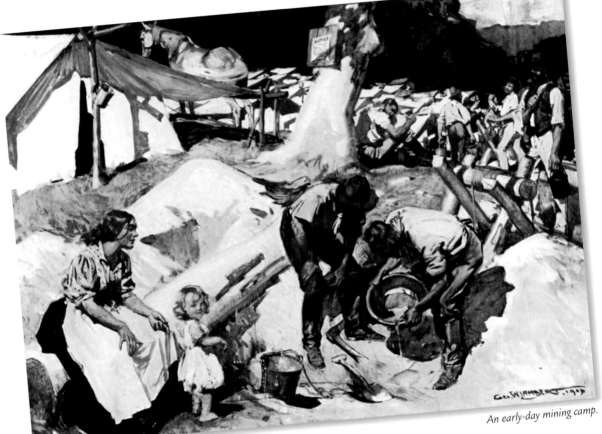

An early-day mining camp.

Healthful, Fertile Oregon

In the late 1830s, the United States suffered a bad economic depression. Farmers' crops were worth less, workers could not earn as much money, and storekeepers did not sell as many goods. At that time, early Christian missionaries to the Oregon country wrote about the fertile Willamette River area there. This was seen as "open" and "unsettled" land, even though many Indians lived there.

Helena, Montana.

The Oregon country was an attractive place. The climate in Oregon was said to be better than the Midwest's. Also, the first few white visitors to Oregon reported no sign of malaria there. Malaria is a severe disease that begins with flu-like symptoms. It is carried by mosquitoes, but at that time no one understood the cause of it. Malaria sickened thousands of people along the Ohio, Mississippi, and lower Missouri rivers every summer.

In 1841, the U.S. government passed a law that allowed citizens to live on open land, build a home and plant crops, and claim the land for their own. They could buy their claim for a very low price as soon as the government surveyed it. Emigrants began moving to Oregon country in large numbers until the Civil War began in 1861.

The California Gold Rush

Americans started traveling to northern California in the 1840s to farm and ranch, but when gold was discovered in 1848, many Americans headed for California to prospect for gold. Many bought tickets on sailing ships that went around the southern tip of South America. Others took boats to Panama, walked across the land, and got on other boats to go to California.

HEAVY TRAFFIC

These ways were expensive, so an equal number of people traveled the overland trails. They went as fast as they could and were known as "gold rushers." People going to California also were called "49ers" because 1849 was the first year that so many people rushed to California.

Pikes Peak or Bust!

Ten years later, gold and silver discoveries drew people to Colorado. Gold was discovered in 1858 in Cherry Creek near present-day Denver and on Cripple Creek near present-day Colorado Springs. Even though Cripple Creek was sixty miles away from Pikes Peak, prospectors heading to Colorado used the slogan "Pikes Peak or Bust!"

At these Colorado sites, gold and silver ran in veins through quartz rock. Expensive mines had to be dug and special furnaces built to get the gold and silver out of the hard quartz. In 1859, 50,000 men rushed to Colorado, but half of them left almost at once because there was not nearly as much loose gold as they had heard.

Emigrants headed to Colorado in 1860.

This painting illustrates how some Americans viewed the westward journey.

Montana Gold Fields

Gold was found in far western Montana in 1862. California prospectors headed east to Montana. Others went west to Montana, traveling the main emigrant trail to Fort Laramie. When the Bozeman Trail opened in 1863 through Sioux hunting lands of the Powder River country in Wyoming and Montana, the Indians attacked enough wagon trains that Americans soon called the trail the "Bloody Bozeman." In 1868, the U.S. government negotiated a treaty with the Sioux to close the trail. After that, the main Montana route was north from the Oregon Trail through Idaho.

Manifest Destiny

Increasing numbers of Americans began moving away from settled states into future Oregon, Texas, New Mexico, and Arizona during the early 1840s. In 1845, a New York newspaper editor named John O'Sullivan wrote that it was the "manifest destiny" of U.S. citizens to spread out. They not only could, but should—he said—fill the continent from the Atlantic Ocean to the Pacific. He had found a catchy term for something many Americans already believed. They thought that farming was a better use for land than hunting on it, as the Indians did. They also wanted to take away Spain's colony of California, and make it part of the United States.

The Platte River Road

The Platte River Road that ran alongside the Platte River's south side was like a divided highway, with mostly one-way traffic. On this busy trail, people often could see more than a hundred wagons by day—and campfires by night.

Trails to Oregon

Oregon-bound emigrants traveled west from the Platte River Road across the Rocky Mountains, where they came upon a beautiful valley, the Grand Ronde, with good water and plenty of grass. After difficult passages over the Columbia River and the Cascade Mountains, the emigrants arrived in Oregon City and the lush Willamette Valley.

The Mormon Trail

The first Mormon emigrants, led by Brigham Young in 1847, drove their wagon train along the Platte River's north side, which became known as the "Mormon Trail." After crossing the Rocky Mountains, Mormon trains headed south through Wyoming into the Great Salt Lake Valley.

California Trails and Cutoffs

At Fort Hall, California-bound emigrants left the Oregon Trail and headed southwest to cross the Sierra Nevada Mountains into California. In 1849, the year after gold was discovered, thousands of prospectors rushed to California, creating many new cutoff trails across the Sierra Nevada.

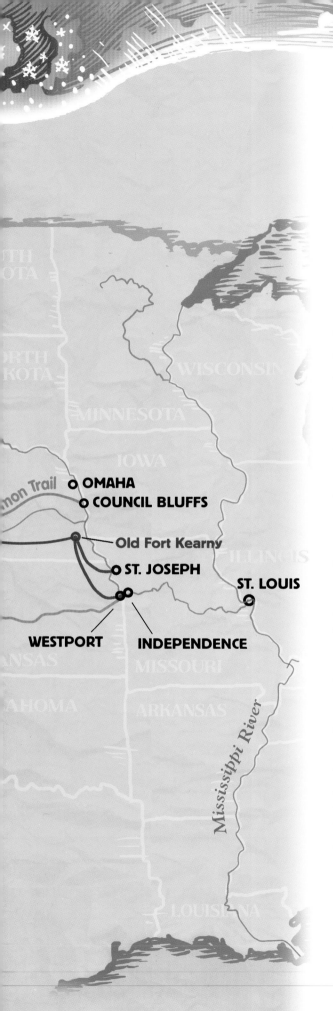

ON Trail
O OMAHA
O COUNCIL BLUFFS

Old Fort Kearny

O ST. JOSEPH

ST. LOUIS

WESTPORT   **INDEPENDENCE**

Mississippi River

3
WHICH WAY DID THEY GO?

Can You Tell Me How to Find Oregon?

There was not just one Oregon Trail or one California Trail, but both ends of the emigrant trails split off in different directions from the main trail. Separate trails from the jumping-off places joined at old Fort Kearny in Nebraska to form one main trail, the Platte River road, that went west up the Platte River to Fort Laramie.

In the Rocky Mountains, the trail divided again. Several trails—the Oregon Trail and the Mormon Trail—went to today's Idaho, Oregon, and Utah.

California-bound emigrants could chose from two main trails across Nevada, and had even more choices for crossing the Sierra Nevada Mountains into California.

> May 31, 1853
>
> Evening—Traveled 25 miles today. When we started this morning there were two large droves of cattle and about 50 wagons ahead of us, and we either had to stay poking behind them in the dust or hurry up and drive past them. It was no fool of a job to be mixed up with several hundred head of cattle and only one road to travel in, and the drovers threatened to drive their cattle over you if you attempted to pass them.
>
> —FROM THE DIARY OF AMELIA STEWART KNIGHT, WHO LEFT IOWA WITH HER FAMILY IN APRIL 1853 AND MADE IT TO OREGON THAT FALL

4

HOW DID THEY GET THERE?

bonnet

wagon bow

jockey box

doubletree

wagon bed

singletree

tongue

hub

brake

grease bucket

iron tire

axle

Emigrant Wagons: The Family Mini-van

Emigrant wagons were smaller, lighter-weight versions of the Conestoga wagons. The wagon boxes had flat bottoms and straight sides. Above the wagon bed, four or five bows held a bonnet made of sailcloth that was varnished for waterproofing. Many emigrants added slogans, such as "California or Bust" or "Smith Family from Wisconsin." Hinged boxes inside held provisions and the floor was crammed with goods a family needed to start a new life. Some wagons had two floors, which provided more storage space, but made the load heavier. Ropes, whips, and other tools were tied

Emigrant Wagon: Just the facts, Ma'am

- Dimensions: 11 feet long by 4 feet wide by 10 feet tall (including wagon cover)
- Oxen Power: 4 oxen or 6 mules
- Weight: 1,300 pounds empty. 3,000 pounds loaded.

underneath or beside the wagon bed. A rubber bag of axle grease hung on the side, along with a barrel of drinking water.

Conestoga Wagons: The Eighteen-Wheeler

Before railroads, Conestoga wagons were the tractor-trailer trucks of the day. They were developed around

1725 in the Conestoga River area of Pennsylvania. These big wagons had boxes with curved bottoms and curved sides to keep the freight from moving around. Cloth tops, held up by curved wooden bows, angled out in front and back to keep the rain off the loads. In the wagon's back, the tops could be closed by a drawstring, and there were flaps or curtains over the front opening. Conestoga wagons were not used by emigrants, though, because they were too large, cumbersome, and required too many oxen or mules.

Conestoga Wagon: Just the facts, Ma'am
- Dimensions: 17 feet long by 8 feet wide by 20 feet tall (including wagon cover)
- Oxen Power: 24 oxen needed
- Weight: 1½ tons empty. 8 tons loaded.

Throwing Things Away

Guidebooks recommended taking 1,600 to 2,000 pounds—about the weight of a buffalo—of provisions, furniture, equipment, and clothing. It was very hard to decide what to leave behind, and many people started with too many things.

MOVING SALE!

But, out on the prairie, the emigrants had to choose between keeping these possessions or reaching their goal at all. As the team animals tired, things were

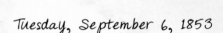

Tuesday, September 6, 1853

Still in camp, washing and overhauling the wagons to make them as light as possible to cross the mountains. Evening—After throwing away a good many things and burning up most of the deck boards of our wagons so as to lighten them, got my washing and cooking done and started on again...camped near the gate or foot of the Cascade Mountains.

—AMELIA STEWART KNIGHT, WHO LEFT IOWA IN 1853 AND MADE IT TO OREGON THAT FALL

Tuesday, July 10, 1866

We are hauled along by four yoke of cattle. Fastened in the front bow of the wagon and waving over us is the "Stars and Stripes" about 3 ft. long, on the bottom of our wagon is heavy machinery filled up with blankets, tobacco &c for the men—canned fruit—a small keg of whiskey... carpet sacks, mess kit &c—the blankets making a comfortable loading place.

—FROM THE DIARY OF THOMAS ALFRED CREIGH, WHO TRAVELED IN ONE OF THE LAST WAGON TRAINS OVER THE BOZEMAN TRAIL

thrown away to lighten the load. Families abandoned all kinds of luxury items to spare their teams—parlor organs, large sofas, wooden chests of drawers, iron stoves, and tall bookshelves. Later emigrants could help themselves to useful items found along the trail—but only if their wagons had room.

Wagon Wheels

The front pair of wheels on the wagons were smaller than the back pair, which helped the wagon turn right or left. Skilled craftsmen called "wheelwrights" made and repaired wheels. A wheelwright carefully shaped and fitted pieces of hardwood into a circle with spokes, then put a tight iron "tire" around the rim. He heated the iron so that it expanded, placed it around the wood, then he plunged the whole wheel into cold water to cool the iron and tighten it.

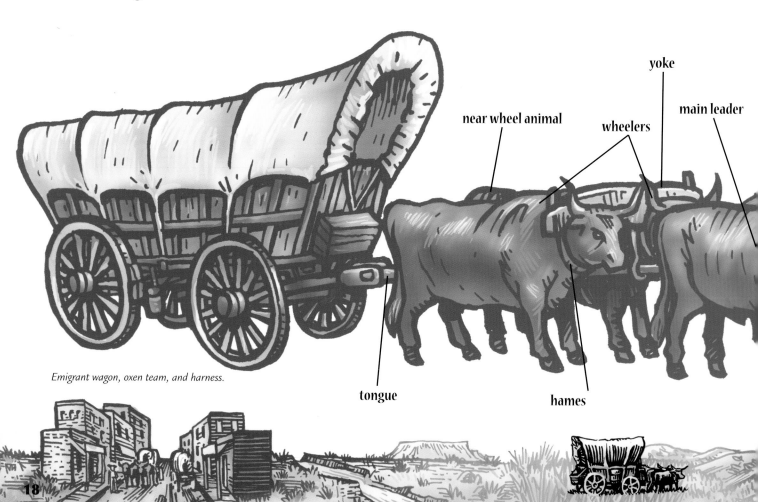

Emigrant wagon, oxen team, and harness.

yoke

near wheel animal

wheelers

main leader

tongue

hames

Cows, mules, and horses hitched together in Kearney, Nebraska.

Oxen, Mules, or Horses?

Six out of ten animals pulling emigrant wagons were oxen. Other teams had mules, which were sturdy but more expensive. Horses were rarely used. An ox cost $25 at that time, but a mule was three times that much! Mules could be stubborn and hard to manage, but oxen were more likely to become "spooked," or frightened, and try to stampede.

Fixing a "Flat"

On the hot prairie and in the dry mountain climates, the wooden wheels shrank and came loose from the iron tires. People stuffed wedges of wet rawhide into the gaps. This untanned hide hardened as it dried and made the tires fit tightly again.

leaders

Team Spirit

A driver placed his animals with great care. He guided the main leader, the right-hand animal, by the "jerk line" attached to its collar. To turn left, the driver gave one long pull to the jerk line and shouted "Gee!" When the driver made several short jerks and shouted "Haw!" the leader turned right. When the jerk line

Walking West

Most emigrants walked beside their wagons to spare the animals the effort of pulling their weight, too. When they did ride, it was a bone-rattling experience. Occasionally, women or children would nap in the moving wagons during hot summer afternoons. If the man of the family got sick, he rode in the wagon while someone else guided the team. People of the famous Mormon "handcart brigades" of 1856 through 1860 pushed or pulled small wooden carts—and even wheelbarrows—that carried supplies and belongings. They had to take even less than emigrants who had wagons.

The Dollar Then and Now

Prices given in this book are what things cost during the years from 1840 to 1860. But $1.00 in 1850 equals $23.40 in 2005! In 1860, a novel or a haircut was 10¢. A children's chemistry set was $10.

Unskilled workers in the United States were happy to earn $1.00 for a day's work. Skilled workers, like carpenters, earned $2.00 a day. Male teachers earned nearly $13.00 a month, but female teachers were paid only $5.00.

moved and the rings jingled, the other animals knew the leader would show them which way to turn. Most of the time, the driver walked beside the left-hand wheeler, or "near wheel" animal, or rode that animal with a light saddle.

Drivers cracked leather whips over the teams' heads as a signal. They did not use their whips to hit their precious animals.

Two is Better than One

If they got stuck in mud or had to climb a steep hill, emigrants practiced "double-teaming." Emigrants from one wagon borrowed the team from another wagon. Both teams pulled the wagon out of the mud or up to the top. Then they both were hitched to the lender's wagon to pull it up a mountain or out of the mud. Unhitching and rehitching the teams took a long time, so the wagon train did not go far on days when they had to help each other out.

Cut Out that Racket!

Wagon trains were noisy. Wooden wagons creaked, and harness chains jingled. People hung metal cooking utensils on the outside, and those clanged and banged with every bump. Wagon wheels had to be greased so they didn't squeak. Plenty of times the grease wore off before people were able to stop. Horses and mules neighed, and oxen bellowed. Chickens squawked from their cages, and cows mooed. Adults and children shouted to each other.

This racket drove wild animals, including bison, away from the trails. Both emigrants and Indians had to hunt farther and farther from the noisy wagon trains when they wanted fresh meat.

Circling the Wagons

Most people slept in tents. During storms, they could crowd into the packed wagons for shelter, but it was not a comfortable night. On many wagon trains, the emigrants pulled their wagons into a large circle or square at day's end. They unhitched the teams and turned the animals loose in this temporary "corral."

MORE INFO

Hard stretches of the trail were littered with piles of "leeverites" — items the emigrants had to "leave 'er right here" to lighten their wagons.

Mormon emigrants and handcarts near Fort Bridger.

5
WHAT DID THEY TAKE?

Approximate Cost Per Pound of the Basic Foods in 1850

Shopping list

flour	2¢
cornmeal	5¢
bacon	5¢
sugar	4¢
coffee	10¢
tea	60¢
vinegar	25¢
salt	6¢
baking soda	12¢
rice	5¢
dried beans	6¢
dried fruit	6¢
total	= $1.46

Emigrant Grocery List

Basic List (for Four People)

824 pounds of flour

80 pounds of cornmeal

725 pounds of bacon

200 pounds of lard or suet (rendered at home)

160 pounds of sugar

75 pounds of coffee

10 gallons of vinegar (to soak tough meat and also prevent scurvy)

25 pounds of salt

2 pounds of baking soda

200 pounds of dried beans

60 pounds of dried fruit

20 pounds of rice

Extras

Rare treats: canned milk, fruits and vegetables

A Walking Dairy Farm

Cows walked along with the emigrant trains across the continent, and some families tied chicken cages onto the outside of their wagons. As long as they could keep their animals alive, these people had fresh milk and eggs. Other emigrants carefully packed eggs into their flour barrels.

Campsite in the Rocky Mountain foothills.

May 23, 1866

Perhaps you would like to know what we have at our meals...We sometimes boil potatoes...We then pick up some codfish and cook it with milk. Billy usually washes the potatoes and gets them cooking and I make a large batch of biscuit....

We have tea for supper—take the end board of our large wagon...put it across our two provision boxes, put around our tin plates, cups and knives and forkes, set our spider of fish on the table, and the kettle of potatoes either on it or by the side of it, set on our dripper of biscuit, butter, etc...For breakfast we have coffee and warm some of the biscuit baked the night before.

—ELLEN "NELLIE" GORDON FLETCHER

Cooking supplies included cooking utensils, a churn, a dutch oven, tin plates and cups, baking pans, a water keg, a coffee pot, and buckets.

Personal items included a medicine chest, picture album, the Bible, or treasures, such as a favorite doll.

Weapons included rifles and pistols as well as gunpowder, lead, and shot.

Food items included pounds of bacon, lard, coffee, flour, rice, sugar, and tea carried in sacks and barrels.

Clothing included two changes of clothing, flannel underwear, sunbonnets, cowhide boots, a heavy overcoat, two pairs of walking shoes, and cotton and wool socks.

Household supplies included blankets, quilts, candles, school books, sewing supplies, soap, and a washboard.

Tools recommended for the trail were axes, augers, a bull whip, wrenches, screwdrivers, spokes, chains, ox and horse shoes, hammers, a rope, and matches in a corked bottle.

The emigrants' lips blistered and split in the dry air, and their only remedy was to rub axle grease on their lips.

Churning on the Road

Emigrants who had fresh milk put it into their butter churns or buckets in the morning. They hung the containers on the wagon's shady side and let the wagon's bumping do the churning. That separated the milk into fresh butter and buttermilk.

Eagle Rock and Scotts Bluff, emigrant trail landmarks.

6
WHAT WAS LIFE LIKE ON THE TRAIL?

Independence on the Plains. Gathering Chips

Women and children collected buffalo chips for fuel.

Wake Up, Sleepyhead!

Days started early on the trail, about 4:00 A.M. In some wagon trains, a rifle was fired or a trumpet was blown to wake everyone. Men checked at once to see that no animals had strayed away. Women started fires and began cooking breakfast, which took a couple of hours. If the party had brought cows, these needed to be milked. After eating, everyone helped take down the tents

and repack the wagon. The teams were hitched to the wagons, and by 7:00 A.M. the train moved out.

Story Problem

An ox-drawn wagon traveled about two miles per hour. The trip from western Iowa or Missouri to Oregon or California was about 2,000 miles long. To drive that far in a car going 60 miles per hour, it takes 33 hours and 20 minutes, or approximately four 8-hour days. How long did it take the emigrants?

Answer: Ox-drawn wagons took 1,000 hours, or 4 months!

Dutch Ovens

Emigrants found many uses for cooking kettles called Dutch ovens. Made of heavy iron, Dutch ovens have a short handle on each side and short legs on the bottom. They could be filled with bread dough and placed over, or buried in, the fire's coals or be hung on tripods above the fire. The emigrant's Dutch ovens were much larger than the ones we use today.

Your Chore? Gather Buffalo Poop

Cooking was done over an open fire. An emigrant built a fire in a shallow trench to protect the flames from the wind. The main fuel was the dried dung of bison, called "buffalo chips." Other fuels were hardened plant roots or sagebrush.

Two to three bushels of buffalo chips were needed to cook a meal. During the day, women and children carried sacks and gathered the lightweight chips as they walked beside the wagons.

Clean Your Plate!

A big, hot breakfast early in the morning was important before starting the day's hard work. In the middle of the day, wagon trains stopped for one or two hours for what they called "dinner." This was mostly to rest the teams. People ate left-overs from the evening before. Supper came after the day's travel ended, around 5:00 P.M.

Bacon and Bread Again?

Most people ate bread and bacon, and drank coffee—day after day. One woman wrote that the only change from "bread and bacon" was to "bacon and bread."

The bacon they ate was mostly fat, with tiny slivers of lean meat. Some people stuck twigs through their pieces of bacon and cooked it like marshmallows over the coals. Bread was made of flour or corn meal and cooked in a Dutch oven, or patted into cakes and placed on hot rocks at the edge of the campfire.

Some people took rice and dried beans, which needed plenty of water and a long time to cook. These foods worked best when the wagon train stopped for a layover. Wild berries were a big treat when they were ripe.

September 4, 1887

Dear Aunt,

...I kept neglecting writing to see whether we were going to stay here or not but we are not going to stay here now. We have concluded to go on through to oregon this fall....If it was not so cold, I think we would like here...Game is plenty deer & Elk, Bear. The men are going out on a big Hunt before we start out again. They will bring in a wagon load of game in (which) you never saw the like of fish in your life, mostly all Trout, they are right spoted.

From your Neice,
M. Zemmer

—LETTER OF MOLLIE ZEMMER, WRITTEN IN THE SUMMER OF 1887

Monday, August 1, 1853

Still in camp, have been waiting all day, and all hands have had all the wild currants they could eat, they grow in great abundance along the river. There are three kinds, red, black, and yellow.

—AMELIA STEWART KNIGHT

Food on the Hoof

When they could, men hunted either bison or pronghorns (which they called "antelope") for fresh meat, as well as sage hens and wild hares. Favorite bison parts were the

Monday, June 27, 1853

Cold, cloudy and very windy...the men have just got their breakfast over and drove up the stock. It is all hurry and bustle to get things in order. It's children milk the cows, all hands help yoke these cattle, the d—l's in them. Plutarch answers, "I can't, I must hold the tent up, it is blowing away"... "Seneca, don't stand there with your hands in your pockets. Get your saddles and be ready."

—AMELIA STEWART KNIGHT

tongues and the humps, which were cooked and eaten at once.

Most of the meat was "jerked," or dried in the sun, so that it would keep. People strung ropes along the wagon covers and hung the meat to dry as they moved along. Hanging up the meat was a chore often assigned to children. Dust and insects stuck to the meat and had to be rinsed off before eating.

Where the Buffalo Roam

American bison, what we often call "buffalo," still roamed the prairies in herds of thousands from Nebraska to the Rocky Mountains when the emigrant trains rolled past. Most of the time, bison walked calmly along, eating and stopping to drink at water holes. But when something frightened them—such as lightning—they stampeded, thundering across the prairie until the ground felt like it was shaking. On the wide-open prairie, however, they could easily run around the wagons. These hoofed animals with thick brown coats, weigh nearly 2,000 pounds and stand six feet tall.

Dividing Up Chores

At home, cooking, washing, and laundry were women's work. Besides working on their farms or at their trades, men tended the family's livestock, chopped firewood, and drove the buggy or wagon.

Life on the trail was different. People did what needed to be done. Everyone helped with the laundry. If a man became ill, his wife drove their wagon. Men helped unpack the tents and bedding for nightly camps. Some women learned to shoot rifles, and those who were good shots went hunting.

WATCH FOR WORKERS

How to Wash Clothes in the 1850s
(Or Why Washing Machines were Invented!)

Wagon trains took a laundry layover every two weeks. (At home, people did laundry once a week). Here are the time-consuming steps:

1. Gather water from the river.
2. Gather wood or bison chips to make a fire.
3. Boil water.
4. Scrape slivers of soap into hot water.
5. Scrub clothes against washboard.
6. Wring soap out of clothes.
7. Rinse in hot water.
8. Repeat step 7.
9. Boil in fresh water to remove soap or lice.
10. Hang on bushes to dry.
11. Fold and store without ironing.

New-Fangled Clothing

Walking over the dusty prairie and cooking over campfires was not easy for women who wore the hooped skirts and corsets that were fashionable at the time. Later emigrant women wore the new "Bloomer costume." In 1851, a woman named Amelia Jenks Bloomer suggested that women stop binding their waists into corsets and wear looser jackets, shorter skirts, and very baggy trousers—with elastic at the ankles.

Amelia Jenks Bloomer, inventor of the loose trousers known as bloomers.

Having Fun

When they relaxed during the evenings and layovers, emigrants played cards, checkers, or chess—games that were lightweight and easy to pack. Children in a wagon train played games such as Button, Button or Drop the Handkerchief. Perhaps someone had brought a violin and played music for singing and even dancing. Popular songs of the day were "Old Dan Tucker," "Buffalo Gals," and Stephen Foster's "Oh, Susannah" and "Sewanee River." The 49ers (gold rushers headed for California) especially liked to sing the silly "Oh, My Darling Clementine."

Try Out Emigrant Children's Games

Button, Button: Have your friends sit in a semicircle, holding their hands out, palms together. You are "it." You hold a button between your palms and move from person to person, sliding your hands between each player's palms. Leave the button in someone's hand, but keep on going, pretending to give the button to each player. When you are finished, call out, "Button, button, who's got the button?" The one who guesses which person has the button is "it."

Drop the Handkerchief: Have your friends form a circle, holding hands. If you are "it," you walk slowly around the outside of the circle, holding a handkerchief, and chanting:

> A tisket, a tasket,
> a green and yellow basket.
>
> I wrote a letter to my love and on the way I dropped it;
>
> A little child picked it up and put it in her pocket.

Cokeville Wyoming Territory
August 13, 1887

Dear Aunt,
We have traveled a good long distance since I wrote you as we are now in Wyoming Territory, just stoped a while to rest our teams & Pa got in to work…Aunt I like this country very wel but we are going on to Oregon in a few weeks Pa cant stop until he gets thare…It is pretty wild out here is the worst objections I have but I guess as the country settles up they will become more civilized…. Good By
I Remaine as ever your Affectionate Neice,
Mollie Zemmer

—LETTER OF MOLLIE ZEMMER, WRITTEN IN THE SUMMER OF 1887

You drop the handkerchief behind a player and run. The second player grabs the handkerchief and chases you around the circle. If you reach the empty space first, the new person is now "it."

Takin' a Break

The wagons needed to keep moving steadily, but they also had to stop for "layovers." This meant staying at the same camp for a whole day. A layover was a time for doing hard work, chores that could not be completed during evening stops.

The wagon train might have to stop at any time for major wagon or harness repairs. Some trains stopped every Sunday. Fording a river or going through a bad rainstorm sometimes meant that all the clothing, bedding, and belongings got wet. The wagons had to be unloaded and their contents spread out in the sun to dry.

The Oregon Trail stretches 547 miles across Oregon. It was the final leg of a long and tiresome journey for those who crossed to the Oregon country on the overland trails.

The W. Jennings General Store and Overland Mail office in the 1850s in Salt Lake City, Utah.

Store and Overland Mail Cos. G. S. L. City.

The goal of the Pony Express (1860–1861) was to deliver a letter in ten days. The fastest delivery on record was President Lincoln's Inaugural Address, which took seven days and seventeen hours to get from St. Joseph to Sacramento, California.

Getting the News

During the four or more months on the trail, people had almost no way to get news from back home. But emigrants often met other trains that had started later, or from a different jumping-off place. They eagerly asked for news—and passed on what they had heard from turnarounds. Or they might meet and visit with soldiers traveling on duty.

After 1844, this word-of-mouth system was nick-named the "prairie telegraph." That date was when Samuel Morse demonstrated his new invention—the telegraph—that could transmit messages by electric signals. The first actual telegraph line did not cross the plains until late in 1861.

Hey, Mr. Postman

MAIL STOP AHEAD

If a wagon train met a turnaround party, its members quickly wrote letters for the turnarounds to mail when they reached a real post office. If they met an army troop, emigrants located soldiers willing to carry their letters to the next fort's post office. Mail from army forts was picked up every two to four weeks. Emigrants' letters took months to be delivered.

When they reached a military or trading fort along the trails, emigrants stood in line to ask whether any letters were waiting there for them. Post offices were crowded and chaotic when a wagon train pulled in.

Sometimes emigrants invented their own post offices. In an abandoned log cabin at Ash Hollow, Nebraska, emigrants tacked up messages with their names, and left letters, hoping that anyone heading east would carry them to the next true post office.

July 25, 1864

Two men, french guides formerly of Capt. Townsend's Train, who were on their way to the Platte river are with us tonight. They took several letters with them belonging to our men, [charging] fifty cents each for conveying them.

—From the diary of Richard Owens, a miner who traveled from Omaha, Nebraska, to Idaho

7
WHAT DID THE EMIGRANTS ENCOUNTER?

Nearly one of every thirty people who started west died along the trail. Although people feared everything from Indian attacks to tornadoes, the biggest dangers on the trails were accidental shootings, followed by drownings and illnesses. Most gunshot wounds happened when someone handled his gun carelessly and shot himself.

Getting Sick

If emigrants got sick, they had to rely on their own remedies because few wagon trains had doctors, and in those days, doctors did not have many medicines for serious illnesses. Scurvy, cholera, and rabies were the most dangerous illnesses emigrants faced.

Scurvy comes from lack of vitamin C, which is found in fresh fruits and vegetables. Although emigrants ate dried fruit and wild berries to prevent scurvy, some developed symptoms of the illness, such as bleeding gums, easy bruising, and wounds that were slow to heal.

Cholera is caused by bacteria that live in water or milk contaminated by human or animal waste. It is like a very, very bad flu—and can kill people in 24 hours.

Rabies comes from the bite of an infected animal, especially dogs, coyotes, and bats.

Cholera

Cholera crept silently, caused by unsanitary conditions: people camped amid garbage left by previous parties picked up the disease and then went about unknowingly spreading it themselves. People in good spirits in the morning could be in agony by noon and dead by evening.

Symptoms started with a stomach ache that grew to intense pain within minutes. Then came diarrhea and vomiting that quickly dehydrated the victim. Within hours the skin was wrinkling and turning blue. If death did not occur within the first 12 to 24 hours, the victim usually recovered.

An emigrant with rabies would die in 10 days. Today, people exposed to rabies are treated with six vaccine shots given over 28 days.

Comin' Down the Mountain

Double-teaming helped emigrants climb up steep trails, but going down steep slopes was also difficult. Early wagons had no brakes, and when a simple brake was added, it slowed only one wheel. A runaway wagon that crashed down a hill could destroy the emigrants' animals, food, and belongings.

To slow their wagons, people unhitched all their horses but one pair, just enough to guide the wagon. Then they sent one wagon downhill at a time, while men pulled back on ropes tied to the wagon. Sometimes they dragged logs from the backs of their wagons or put metal chains around the outside of the wagon wheels for traction. They also tied up the wheels so that they slid over the ground like sled runners.

Those with ox teams would hitch all but one yoke behind the wagon. The oxen did not like having that wagon in front of them and tried to pull away from it. That turned them into animal "brakes."

> June 10, 1866
>
> There is a large family [that] had been obliged to lie by on account of an accident which happened to a little child four years old. He fell out of the wagon and the wheels ran over his head and thigh. His head was badly cut and his thigh broken. They had been there several days and the little boy was getting better. He is a sweet little fellow, and reminded me of Rollo.
>
> —Ellen "Nellie" Gordon Fletcher

> ### Sickness on the Trail
>
> Mother was...rapidly failing under her sorrows. The nights and morning were very cold and she took cold from the exposure...With camp fever and a sore mouth, she fought bravely against fate for the sake of her children, but she was soon bed-fast.
>
> —From Across the Plains in 1844 by Catherine Sager Pringle

Danger! River Crossing Ahead!

Crossing rivers was one of the most dangerous things that emigrant wagons had to do. At some places, people drove their wagons across shallow spots in the rivers called "fords." On deep rivers, emigrants built rafts to float themselves and their wagons across. The livestock had to swim. A person might ride one animal, using it to guide the others.

In a few places, earlier settlers had built crude wooden ferries tied to guide ropes to take wagons and people across. A ferryman moved the raft by pushing a long pole against the river bottom. Ferry owners charged high prices—from $2.00 to $5.00 to take a wagon across.

Later, toll bridges replaced some ferries. Crossing these was not as expensive, at 15¢ to 50¢ per wagon.

Sunday morning, May 8, 1853

Still in camp waiting to cross. There are three hundred or more wagons in sight and as far as the eye can reach, the bottom is covered, on each side of the river, with cattle and horses. There is no ferry here and the men will have to make one out of the tightest wagon-bed (every company should have a waterproof wagon-bed for this purpose.) Everything must now be hauled out of the wagons head over heels... then the wagons must be all taken to pieces and then by means of a strong rope stretched across the river, with a tight wagon-bed attached to the middle of it, the rope must be long enough to pull from one side to the other, with men on each side of the river to pull it. In this way we have to cross everything a little at a time.

—Amelia Stewart Knight

The Mormon ferry across the North Platte River.

DANGER RIVER XING

The Donner Party

The most famous group of emigrants to be caught by winter was the Donner Party in 1846. Their 20 wagons had left a larger train to try out a new route to California. On October 31, they were near the top of the Sierra Nevada Mountains, when they were trapped by a blizzard in ten feet of snow.

124   *ACROSS THE PLAINS IN THE DONNER PARTY (1846).*

ON THE WAY TO THE SUMMIT.

In mid-December, the first party member died. Fifteen men, women, and children left the camp on homemade snowshoes, trying to get help. They hiked for more than a month, but only seven managed to reach Sutter's Fort. Many people at the mountain camp died from illness and starvation.

Rescuers from Sutter's Fort in California rescued the last camp survivors on April 1, 1847. Of the original 89 party members, only 47 members survived. Some people in the Donner Party ate some of the dead to survive.

James Read, who led the second relief party, described the scene: "There lay the limbs, the skulls, and the hair of the poor beings who had died from want and whose flesh preserved the lives of their surviving comrades...who looked more like demons than human beings." The Donner Party story terrified future emigrants, but the tragedy was never repeated. After that, volunteers in Oregon and California took food and wagons to get travelers of the mountains before winter.

Saturday, April 23, 1853

Still in camp, it rained hard all night and blew a hurricane almost. All the tents were blown down, and some wagons capsized. Evening—It has been raining hard all day; everything is wet and muddy. One of the oxen missing; the boys have been hunting him all day. Dreary times, wet and muddy, and crowded in the tent, cold and wet and uncomfortable in the wagon. No place for the poor children. I have been busy cooking, roasting coffee, etc., today, and have come into the wagon to write this and make our bed.

—AMELIA STEWART KNIGHT

Road Report

Weather was a daily concern for emigrants. Weather conditions determined when the traveling season began and ended. A big rain storm turned the trail into mud and emigrants had to wait for it to dry, so their teams and wagons would not get stuck. Traveling in wooden wagons with cloth tops, with no buildings in sight, meant they were not well protected.

The emigrants' best hope was to start out in mid-April in order to reach Oregon or California by the beginning of September. If a train left the jumping-off place too early, rivers and creeks swollen with smowmelt would be harder to cross and the grass on the plains would not be ready to feed the livestock.

If a train left too late, there would be not be much grass left on the prairie for the livestock. By late August and early September, snow began to fall in the mountains. Crossing the mountains was hard enough without snow blocking the trail.

Dust covered the trail for much of the summer. Emigrants said they "ate dust" all day as everyone walked or drove through the great clouds of dust that rose into the air from animal teams and wagon wheels. Sometimes, to avoid the dust, emigrants took turns as the lead wagon or drove their wagons beside each other instead of in single file.

Rainstorms on the Great Plains are not gentle sprinkles. Sometimes, so much water falls in a short time that the soil cannot absorb it and water rolls across the ground. It is impossible to move through a storm like this—the best thing to do is to wait out the storm in a shelter. The emigrants climbed inside their wagons and closed the cloth tops as tightly as possible.

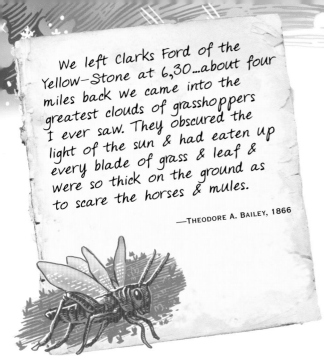

We left Clarks Ford of the Yellow-Stone at 6,30...about four miles back we came into the greatest clouds of grasshoppers I ever saw. They obscured the light of the sun & had eaten up every blade of grass & leaf & were so thick on the ground as to scare the horses & mules.

—THEODORE A. BAILEY, 1866

Mud after rainstorms stuck to the teams' hoofs and the wagons' wheels. Emigrants had to double-team the animals to free their wagons. People sometimes attached ropes to the wagons and pulled right along with the livestock.

Hail fell on the emigrants sometimes—in stones the size of peas, golf balls, or even tennis balls. Hail is formed when rain drops are bounced up and down inside a cloud, in and out of cold air. Layer after layer of water freezes onto each hailstone until it is heavy enough to fall to the ground. The stones were a hazard because they could bruise people and animals that were out in the open. Hail tore the wagons' canvas tops, or even destroyed them.

Stampedes happened when heavy rain or hailstorms made animals—especially oxen—run wildly to try to get away from the storm. Lightning scared them. Hard rain or hail hurt their hides. Some emigrants wrote about having a storm come at night, when the animals were unhitched. By daylight, the oxen, mules, and horses were scattered all over the prairie. Precious time was used to recapture them.

Mosquitoes and gnats appeared during the hot weather. Sometimes tiny gnats were so numerous that emigrants could see black clouds of them coming across the prairie. Smoke rising from their nightly campfires was the only insect repellent emigrants had.

Scorching sun and the accompanying sunburn were another danger as the emigrants crossed the hot, treeless prairie. Wearing hats was the only way the emigrants could protect themselves. Men and boys wore broad-brimmed hats to keep the sun off their faces and necks. Women and girls wore sunbonnets that tied under the chin. These had wide bills that shaded the face, with flaps hanging down to protect the neck.

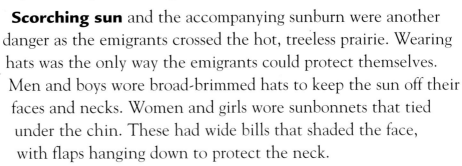

8
WHAT DID THE LAND LOOK LIKE?

The emigrants started their journeys along the Missouri River at elevations less than 500 feet and traveled to spots in Wyoming above 7,000 feet. As the elevation changed, so did the climate, plants, and animals.

THE OREGON WAGON TRAIN
TEX 1959 SERPA WAGONMASTER

Emigrant Graffiti

Emigrants used knives or axle grease to write their names and dates on many of the large rock landmarks along the trails. Although this marred these natural features, the emigrants' graffiti now is part of the historical record. Some people added popular trail slogans: "California or Bust!" and "Pikes Peak or Bust!"

From the western foothills of the Appalachian Mountains to North Platte, Nebraska, 400,000 square miles of tallgrass prairie flourished in the warm moist climate. Wild grasses grew up to eight feet tall—taller than most basketball players. Bison, white-tailed deer, coyotes, beavers, and birds such as bald eagles, lived there.

The land from North Platte, Nebraska, to the Rocky Mountains—once wrongly called the Great American Desert—is today known as the Great Plains. This "semi-arid" ecosystem known as the shortgrass prairie features sagebrush and grasses, such as blue grama, with shallow roots. Prairie dogs, swift foxes, and eagles lived in this habitat.

Scotts Bluff should have an apostrophe. So why doesn't it? The U.S. Board on Geographic Names decided not to use apostrophes in place names so it is easier to read road signs and the small print on maps. This is a big exception to an important punctuation rule!

What Did They See along the Way?

There were a number of landmarks along the trail. At Ash Hollow or Scotts Bluff, for example, emigrants found plenty of water and wood. Imagine the relief they felt at seeing 325-foot-high Chimney Rock—a famous sight that helped them know they

HISTORICAL MARKER

were on the right trail! Landmarks also helped emigrants to time their journey. Emigrants hoped to pass Independence Rock shortly before or after the Fourth of July, so that they could cross the mountains before the snow came.

Some landmarks—such as South Pass—provided an easier way to cross the mountains. Other landmarks, such as The Dalles of the Columbia River, presented a known danger. Early emigrants had to take apart their wagons and tie their belongings onto rafts for the scary, dangerous river ride. Many people drowned. After emigrant Samuel K. Barlow created the Mount Hood Toll Road in 1845 through the Cascade Range to Oregon City, some emigrants chose to pay for the road rather than to risk the river.

> June 15, 1853
>
> Came 19 miles today; passed Independence Rock this afternoon, and cross Sweetwater River on a bridge. Paide 3 dollars a wagon and swam the stock across. The river is very high and swift. There are cattle and horses drowned there every day; there was one cow went under the bridge and was drowned, while we were crossing.
>
> —Amelia Stewart Knight

> Friday, July 8, 1853
>
> We have just left the soda springs, regaling ourselves on soda water. This part of the country is very pretty and quite romantic. We came then on a few miles and stopt at the Steam Boat Springs—a great curiousity, situated near the bank of Bear River. It spouts up about a foot and a half, out of a hole in the solid rock. It is about warm enough to wash in.
>
> —Amelia Stewart Knight

A wagon train pulled by oxen.

WASHINGTON

Fort Vancouver

PORTLAND

Columbia River

MONTANA

Misso

Oregon City

Fort Dalles

The Dalles

Whitman Mission

Shortgrass Prairie

OREGON

Oregon Trail

Oregon Trail

Fort Boise

Fort Hall

DAHO

Soda Springs

Bozeman Trail

Devils Gate

South Pass

Snake River

City of Rocks

Sweetwater River

Fort Laramie

SACRAMENTO

California Trail

Fort Bridger

Independence Rock

North Platte Riv

Chimney Rock

So

Sutter's Fort

NEVADA

SALT LAKE CITY

Laramie Peak

SAN FRANCISCO

CALIFORNIA

UTAH

Ash Hol

PACIFIC OCEAN

ARIZONA

COLORADO

SANTA FE

NEW MEXICO

FORTS

Fort Laramie, near Laramie, Wyoming, was a few adobe buildings when it was purchased by the U.S. Army in 1849. When it was closed in 1890, the fort had 60 wooden buildings and was the site where two important treaties between the U.S. government and the Indians were signed.

Fort Bridger was opened by mountain man Jim Bridger and his partner Louis Vasquez in 1843 and closed in 1890.

Fort Hall, a British fur trading post, was the place where west-bound and south-bound emigrants parted company.

Fort Boise, near Boise, Idaho, was originally a fur-trading post that was rebuilt by the U.S. Army in 1862.

Fort Dalles was built in 1850 by the U.S. Army near an 1820 fur-trading fort to protect Oregon Trail emigrants.

Oregon City, a village of 1,000 people, was the end of the trail for many Oregon-bound emigrants.

Fort Vancouver started with a Hudson's Bay Company trading post that opened in 1825; the U.S. Army set up its own fort in 1849.

Sutter's Fort was established by Swiss immigrant John Sutter in 1839 as New Helvetia on 48,000 acres awarded him by the Spanish colonial government. He raised cattle, raised produce, and trapped fur-bearing animals.

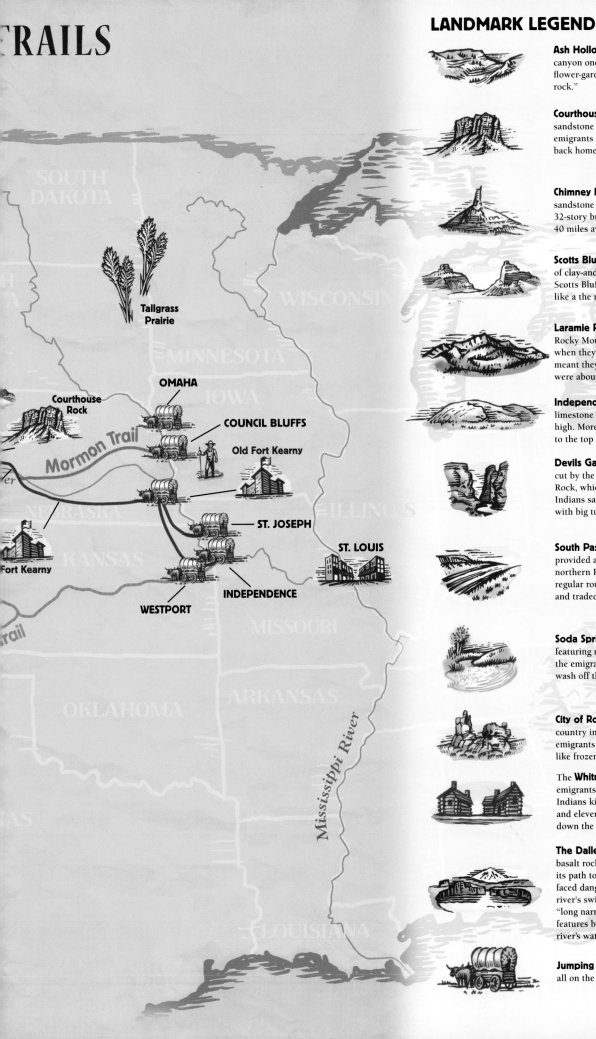

RAILS

SOUTH DAKOTA

WISCONSIN

MINNESOTA

IOWA

Tallgrass Prairie

Courthouse Rock

OMAHA

COUNCIL BLUFFS

Mormon Trail

Old Fort Kearny

NEBRASKA

ILLINOIS

ST. JOSEPH

ST. LOUIS

KANSAS

Fort Kearny

INDEPENDENCE

WESTPORT

MISSOURI

Trail

OKLAHOMA

ARKANSAS

Mississippi River

LOUISIANA

LANDMARK LEGEND

Ash Hollow was a deep, four-mile-long canyon one traveler described as a "pretty flower-garden, walled in by huge piles of rock."

Courthouse Rock is a large block of sandstone and clay that reminded emigrants of their county courthouses back home.

Chimney Rock is a tower of clay and sandstone that rises to the height of a 32-story building and can be seen from 40 miles away.

Scotts Bluff is a rock formation in a group of clay-and-sandstone badlands called the Scotts Bluffs that emigrants said looked like a the ruins of an ancient city.

Laramie Peak was the first peak of the Rocky Mountains that the emigrants saw when they arrived at Fort Laramie—which meant they had crossed the plains and were about 7,200 feet above sea level.

Independence Rock is a rounded limestone formation that rises 128 feet high. More than 5,000 emigrants climbed to the top to mark their names on the rock.

Devils Gate was a deep, narrow canyon cut by the Sweetwater River through Devils Rock, which the Shoshone and Arapaho Indians said was carved by a large beast with big tusks.

South Pass was a wide, open pass that provided an easier route to cross the northern Rocky Mountains. It was a regular route for men who trapped furs and traded with the Indians.

Soda Springs is a cluster of springs featuring naturally bubbly water where the emigrants found a great place to wash off the dust of their journeys!

City of Rocks juts up from shortgrass country in what is now Idaho and emigrants thought the rocks in it looked like frozen fountains of water.

The **Whitman Mission** welcomed emigrants from 1843 until the Cayuse Indians killed the missionaries and eleven other whites and burned down the mission in 1847.

The Dalles featured high banks of black basalt rock choking the Columbia River on its path to the Pacific Ocean. The emigrants faced dangerous river rides along the river's swift, choppy "short narrows" and "long narrows." Today we cannot see these features because dams have raised the river's water level.

Jumping Off Places. These towns are all on the Missouri River.

9

WHOM DID THEY MEET ON THE WAY?

Indians Living near the Trails

Most meetings between Indians and wagon trains were friendly, even if the emigrants and the native people did not understand each other. Newspapers and some emigrant guidebooks often made it sound like every wagon train was attacked by Indians. Some fights occurred, but most Indians approached wagon trains to sell or buy things.

VISITORS PARKING

Plains and Plateau Indians

Plains Indians refers to the different Indian nations who lived on the Great Plains. These people depended on the horse for travel. During the summer, the Indians located their camps near the bison herds. The tribes depended on the buffalo for food, shelter, clothing, and tools. The men hunted and the women preserved meat for winter by drying it. They tanned the buffalo hides into leather and left hair on some hides to make warm winter clothing, blankets, and shoes. Bones were made into tools. Bladders and stomachs became waterproof bags. Horns and hooves were used for containers. Women and children also gathered wild fruits and dried them to eat in their winter village.

E-We-Tone-My, a Nez Perce girl.

Plateau Indians lived west of the Rocky Mountains in what is called the Columbia Plateau. They had horses, but they did not have bison herds to hunt. They based their diet on salmon and other fish, vegetables they raised, and wild roots and fruits. They used grass to weave clothing and containers—and their hats and bowls were so tightly woven that they were waterproof! They wove grass mats to sit on and large mats that became the walls of their wood-framed homes. The emigrants were happy to trade with Plateau Indians for corn, peas, potatoes, pumpkins, onions, and salmon.

July 7–12, 1864

We have stopt here all this day, awaiting trains in so that we may get a large company to go to the Bozeman route. We have now in campe about one hundred, 50 waggon...One poor woman crying and did not wish to come along with us, finaly she consented...Water very bad indeed.

—FROM THE DIARY OF RICHARD OWENS, WHO TRAVELLED TO MONTANA

Indian Attacks: Fact or Fiction?

There is no record of a big Indian attack on a wagon train until the 1860s. Before that, small fights had caused the deaths of a few individuals. In 1862, though, prospectors started using a new trail—the Bozeman Trail—from Fort Laramie in Wyoming north to Montana, which cut right through Sioux hunting lands.

The Sioux led by Chief Red Cloud attacked wagon trains on the Bozeman Trail many times. The U.S. Army built several forts to protect the trains. But, after six years of being defeated by the Sioux, the government closed the trail. The Sioux burned down the abandoned forts.

ROAD ENDS

WANTED! FRESH TEAMS

Give Me Your Tired, Your Poor...Oxen

Trading post owners bought the emigrants' weary animals, cared for them, and fed them throughout the fall, winter, and spring. The following summer, new wagon trains came along and traded their tired animals for the healthy ones from the previous year.

Soldiers, Traders, and Missionaries

After leaving their jumping-off places, emigrants did not see any more towns. The few trading posts and army forts scattered along the way became important places to stop. Emigrants could stop and rest, trade in tired livestock for fresh animals, as well as make a long-awaited trip to the post office for news from home.

Trading and Gift-Giving

Most Indians who approached wagon trains came to trade or to receive gifts. Giving presents to welcome visitors was important in native cultures. Indians naturally thought the wagon trains would have gifts for them as well for crossing their land and making hunting more difficult. Emigrants did not understand, however, and many saw the Indians as "beggars." Many emigrants traded beads, needles, or fishing hooks with the Indians for moccasins, dried roots, and fruits.

Fort Laramie was a major stop on the Emigrant Trail. In 1843, 1,000 emigrants visited the fort. In 1852, more than 50,000 stopped by! At Fort Bridger, emigrants could purchase basic foods and tools, and repair their wagons at the blacksmith shop.

Forts, too, served as landmarks. Fort Hall trading post was important because it was the last post before wagons parted company. Those bound for Oregon Territory headed west. California emigrants turned south toward the Humboldt River in Nevada. By the time most emigrants arrived at Fort Boise, it was mid-September and they were in a hurry. They had nearly 400 miles to travel and they were worried. Would snow trap them like the Donner Party?

In Oregon country, a rest stop for some tired emigrants was the Whitman Mission. The mission among the Cayuse Indians was established in Oregon country in 1836 by Dr. Marcus Whitman and his bride, Narcissa, with Henry and Elizabeth Spalding and William H. Gray. Whitman led the first train there in 1843. This ended in 1847 when measles broke out and the Cayuse Indians killed the Whitmans and eleven other whites and burned down the mission. Built in 1850 to protect and aid Oregon Trail emigrants, Fort Dalles was closed in 1861, when the flood of wagon trains tapered off.

The End of the Trail

For Oregon-bound emigrants, the end of the trail might have been Oregon City, a village of about 1,000 people that featured four general stores, a leather tannery, two silversmiths, three tailors, two sawmills, two cabinet makers, a brick yard, and a newspaper. Here, emigrants were ready to look around and select the farmland they wanted to settle on.

Emigrants might land farther north at Fort Vancouver, the Oregon country trading post of the Hudson's Bay Company. Dr. John McLoughlin, the company's Chief Factor, or "boss," offered American emigrants medical care, food, tools, and supplies on credit. This went against company policy, but McLoughlin believed that it was the right thing to do. He also wanted to keep the peace with these American newcomers.

Or, they may have gone south to Sutter's Fort in California, which was established by Swiss immigrant John Sutter. From an adobe fort he built on the American River, Sutter traded with arriving wagon trains in the 1840s. Then one of Sutter's workers, James Marshall, was building a sawmill for Sutter in January 1848, when he found loose gold in the water. That was Sutter's ruin. Hundreds of prospectors flooded into the area, moved onto his land, butchered his cattle, and panned for gold. His own workers left to try to find their fortunes in gold. By 1852, John Sutter gave up and moved away.

> Tuesday, June 7, 1853
>
> Rained some last night, quite warm today. Just passed Fort Laramie, situated on the opposite side of the river. This afternoon we passed a large village of Sioux Indians. Numbers of them came around our wagons. Some of the woman had moccasins and beads, which they wanted to trade for bread. I gave the women and children all the cakes I had baked. Husband traded a big Indian a lot of hard crackers for a pair of moccasins.
>
> —Amelia Stewart Knight

> June 20, 1866
>
> This has been a day of events to our train...came to the ford of Piney River which we found very high & dangerous...after crossing one or two of our heavy wagons some smarty proposed lashing two light wagons together but no sooner than they had reached the swiftest & deepest part than the front one broke in the reach & the wheels parted company....I had placed my blankets on this wagon for safety as our wagon was very heavy & as I had the cool satisfaction of seeing them going down stream...about 20 naked Arrapahoes...plunged in the current at the bends of the stream & saved nearly all of the floating property, including my blankets.
>
> —Theodore A. Bailey

10
WHAT DID THEY DO AT TRAIL'S END?

Home sweet home at the end of the trail.

Those who survived the long, hard emigrant trek to the West no doubt celebrated as much as their shrunken savings allowed. Farmers searched for good land in Oregon and Washington to homestead. Miners in California and Nevada followed rumors, looking for creeks loaded with loose gold. The Mormons enjoyed their religious freedom and built towns in future Utah.

Families unpacked their wagons and, at long last, did not have to repack everything again each night. Clothes and bedding could be washed and dried—outdoors, of course, until people built their cabins or houses!

Most of the former emigrants now became settlers, happy to stop traveling and just remember their adventures on the trails. A few wrote books about the experience, and included advice for future emigrants. But mostly they built new homes and lives in the western United States.

September 17, 1853

Evening came 6 miles and have camped in a fence corner by a Mr. Lambert's, about 7 miles from Milwaukie. Turn our stock out to tolerable good feed. A few days later my eighth child was born. After this we picked up and ferried across the Columbia River, utilizing skiff, canoes and flatboat to get across, taking three days to complete. Here husband traded two yoke of oxen for a half section of land with one-half acre planted to potatoes and a small log cabin and lean-to with no windows. This is the journey's end.

—AMELIA STEWART KNIGHT

48